EASY GUITAR
WITH NOTES & TAB

CHART HITS
OF 2018–2019

D0504025

ISBN 978-1-5400-4721-2

HAL•LEONARD®

Visit Hal Leonard Online at
www.halleonard.com

Contact us:
Hal Leonard
7777 West Bluemound Road
Milwaukee, WI 53213
Email: info@halleonard.com

In Europe, contact:
Hal Leonard Europe Limited
42 Wigmore Street
Marylebone, London, W1U 2RN
Email: info@halleonardeurope.com

In Australia, contact:
Hal Leonard Australia Pty. Ltd.
4 Lentara Court
Cheltenham, Victoria, 3192 Australia
Email: info@halleonard.com.au

STRUM AND PICK PATTERNS

This chart contains the suggested strum and pick patterns that are referred to by number at the beginning
of each song in this book. The symbols ⊓ and ∨ in the strum patterns refer to down and up strokes, respectively.
The letters in the pick patterns indicate which right-hand fingers play which strings.

p = thumb
i = index finger
m = middle finger
a = ring finger

For example; Pick Pattern 2
is played: thumb - index - middle - ring

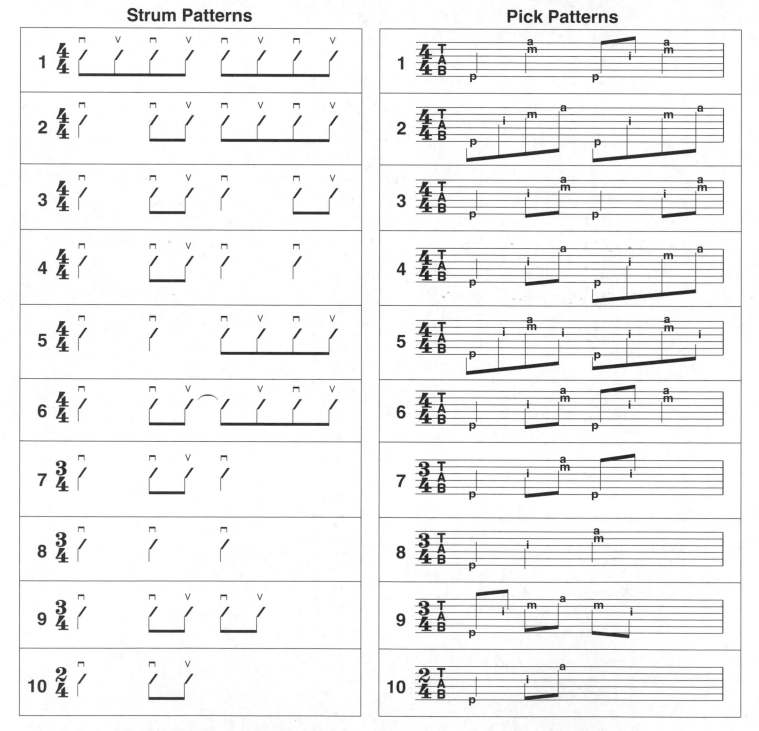

Strum Patterns   **Pick Patterns**

You can use the 3/4 Strum and Pick Patterns in songs written in compound meter (6/8, 9/8, 12/8, etc.).
For example, you can accompany a song in 6/8 by playing the 3/4 pattern twice in each measure.
The 4/4 Strum and Pick Patterns can be used for songs written in cut time (¢) by doubling the note
time values in the patterns. Each pattern would therefore last two measures in cut time.

Broken

Words and Music by Mitchell Collins, Christian Medice and Samantha DeRosa

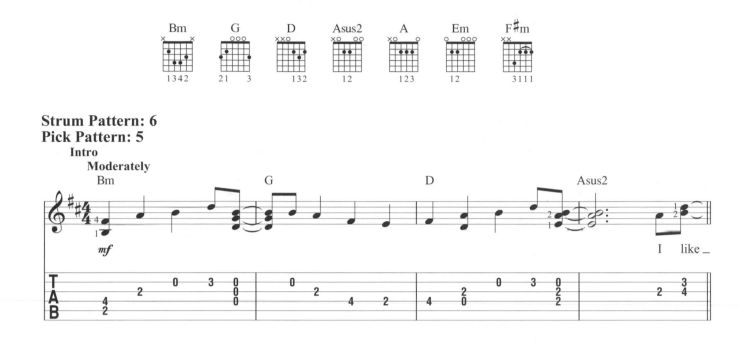

Strum Pattern: 6
Pick Pattern: 5

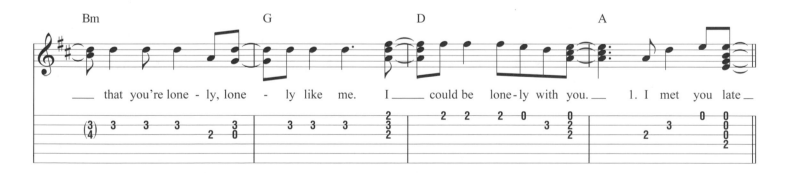

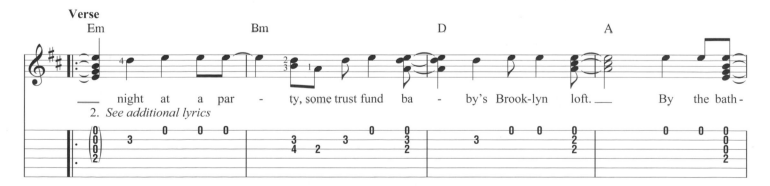

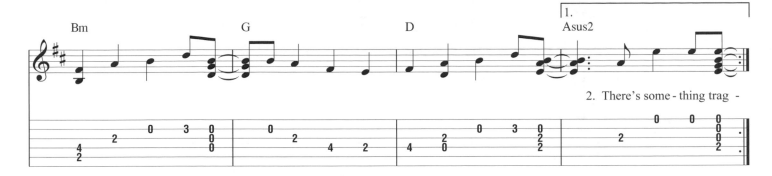

2. There's some-thing trag -

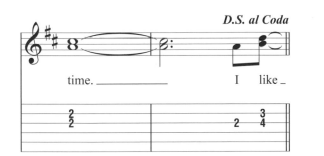

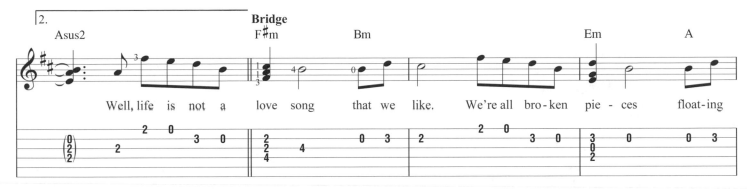

Well, life is not a love song that we like. We're all bro - ken pie - ces float-ing

by. Life is not a love song, we can try to fix our bro - ken pie - ces____ one at a

Coda
Outro

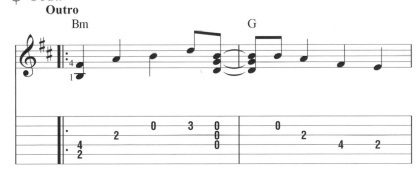

D.S. al Coda

time._____ I like _

Additional Lyrics

2. There's something tragic, but almost pure.
Think I could love you, but I'm not sure.
There's something wholesome, there's something sweet
Tucked in your eyes that I'd love to meet.

Be Alright

Words and Music by Jon Cobbe Hume and Dean Lewis

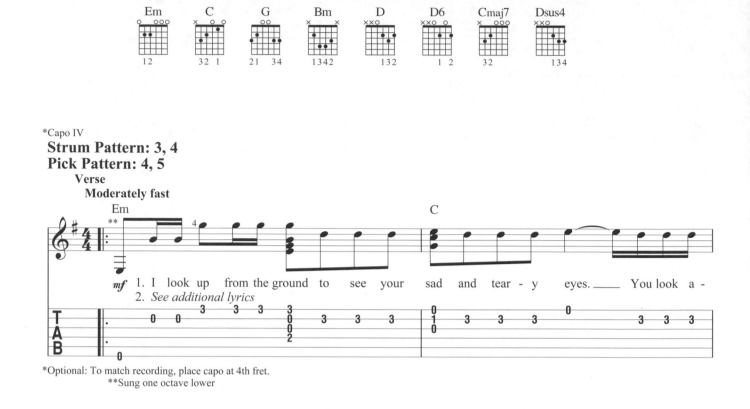

*Capo IV

Strum Pattern: 3, 4
Pick Pattern: 4, 5

Verse
Moderately fast

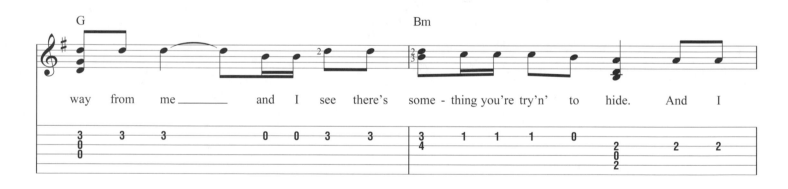

*Optional: To match recording, place capo at 4th fret.
**Sung one octave lower

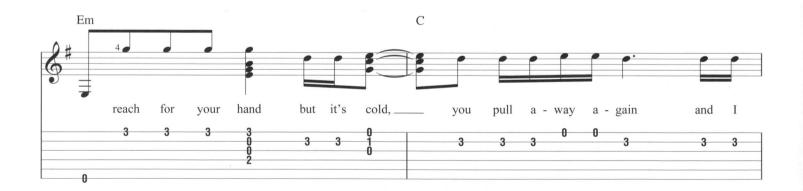

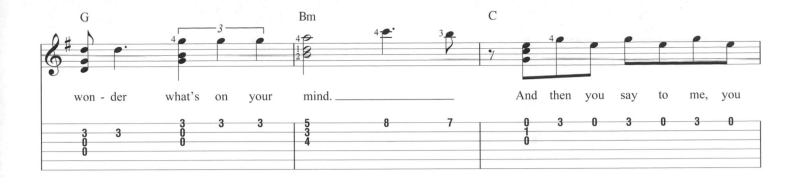

won - der   what's   on   your   mind. _____   And   then   you   say   to   me,   you

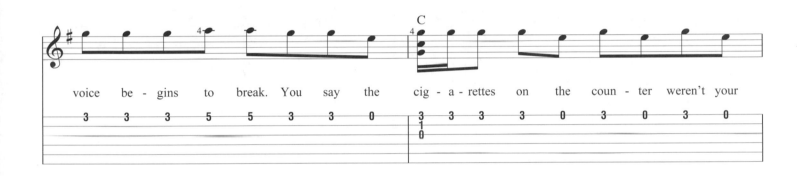

made   a   dumb   mis - take   You   start   to   trem - ble   and   your

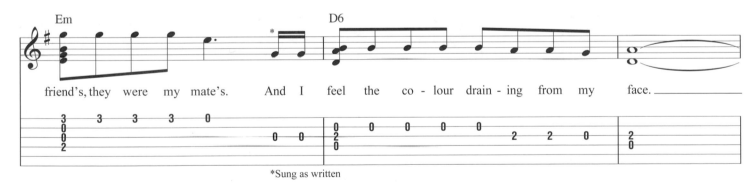

voice   be - gins   to   break.   You   say   the   cig - a - rettes   on   the   coun - ter   weren't   your

friend's, they   were   my   mate's.   And   I   feel   the   co - lour   drain - ing   from   my   face. _____

*Sung as written

𝄋 **Chorus**
Half-time feel

_____   And   my   friends   say: ___   I   know   you   love   her,   but   it's   o - ver,   mate.

It does-n't mat-ter, put the phone a - way.____ It's nev - er eas - y to

walk a - way. Let her go,_____ it-'ll be { 1. al - right. / 2., 3. o - kay. }

It's gon - na hurt for a bit of time ___ so bot - toms up, let's for -

get to - night.____ You'll find an - oth - er and you'll be just fine. Let her

To Coda ⊕

Bridge

go._____ { Noth - ing / noth - ing } heals _____ the

*1st time, let chords ring.

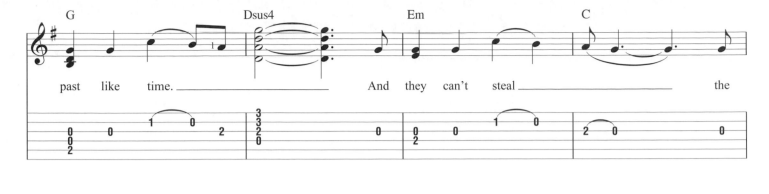

past like time._____ And they can't steal_____ the

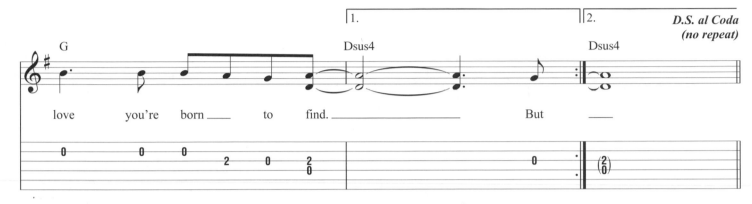

love you're born___ to find._____ But ___

Coda

Outro

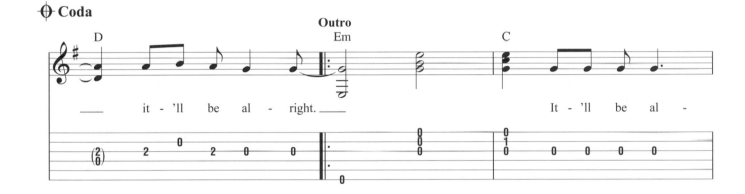

___ it - 'll be al - right.___ It - 'll be al -

right._____ It - 'll be al - right.___ It - 'll be al - right.___

Additional Lyrics

2. So I asked to look back at all the messages you'd sent
And I know it wasn't right, but it was fucking with my head.
And ev'rything deleted like the past, yeah, it was gone.
And when I touched your face, I could tell you're moving on.
But it's not the fact that you kissed him yesterday,
It's the feeling of betrayal that I just can't seem to shake.
And ev'rything I know tells me that I should walk away but I just want to stay.
And my friends say:

Guiding Light

Words and Music by Mumford & Sons

*Strum Pattern: 1
Pick Pattern: 5

*Use Pattern 8 for 3/4 meas.

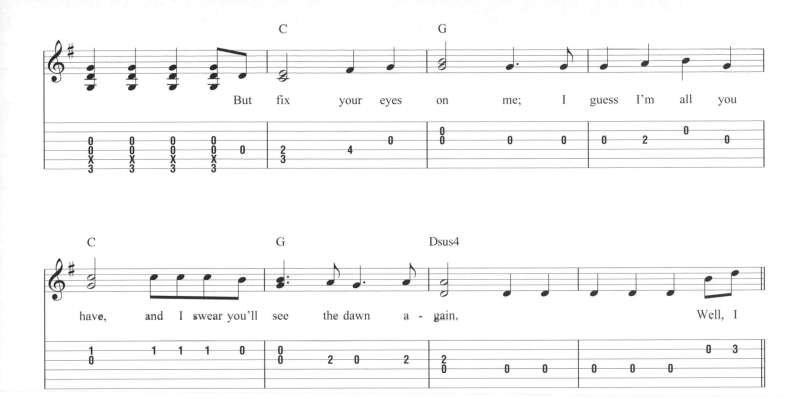

But fix your eyes on me; I guess I'm all you have, and I swear you'll see the dawn a-gain.

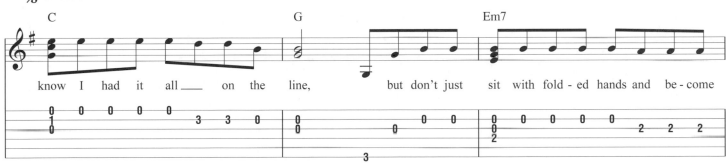

Well, I

Chorus

know I had it all __ on the line, but don't just sit with fold-ed hands and be-come

blind. 'Cause e-ven when there is no star in sight, you'll

To Coda ⊕

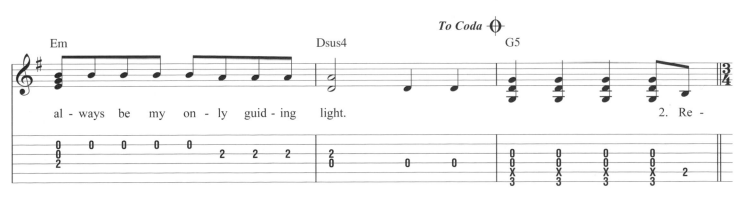

al-ways be my on-ly guid-ing light. 2. Re-

Verse

late to my youth; well, I'm ___ still ___ in awe of you. ___

Dis - cov - er some new truth that was al - ways wrapped a - round

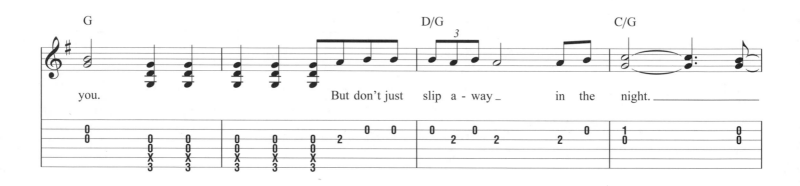

you. But don't just slip a - way ___ in the night. _____

___ But don't just hurl _____ your words ___ from on high.

D.S. al Coda

⊕ Coda

Bridge

Well, I

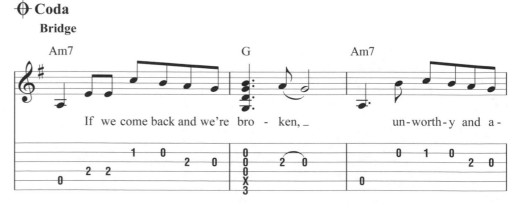

If we come back and we're bro - ken, ___ un - worth - y and a -

shamed, give us some-thing to be - lieve in, ___ and you know we'll go your

way.

'Cause I

Chorus

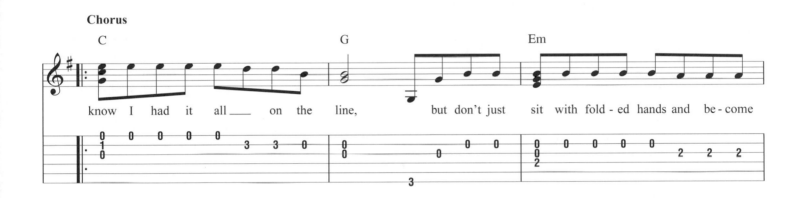

know I had it all ___ on the line, but don't just sit with fold - ed hands and be - come

blind. 'Cause e - ven when there is no star in sight, you'll al - ways be my on - ly guid - ing

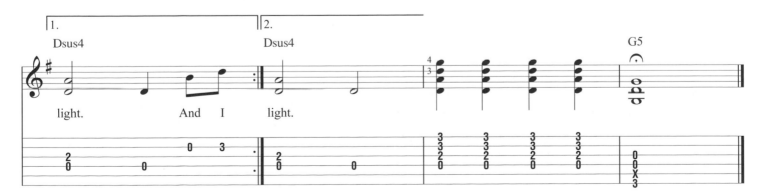

light. And I light.

High Hopes

**Words and Music by Brendon Urie, Samuel Hollander, William Lobban Bean, Jonas Jeberg,
Jacob Sinclair, Jenny Owen Youngs, Ilsey Juber, Lauren Pritchard and Taylor Parks**

*Sung one octave higher.

Had to have high, high hopes for a liv-ing, shoot-ing for the stars when I could-n't make a kill-ing. Did-n't have a dime, but I al-ways had a vi-sion. Al-ways had high, high hopes. _____ Had to have high, high hopes for a

liv - ing. Did - n't know how, but I al - ways had a feel - ing I was gon - na

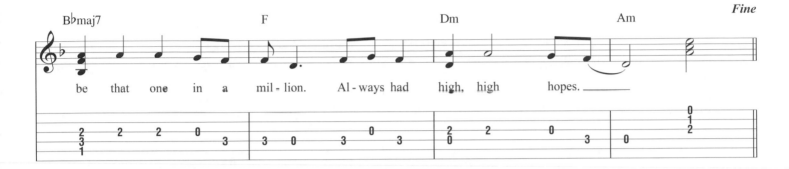

Fine

be that one in a mil - lion. Al - ways had high, high hopes. _____

Verse

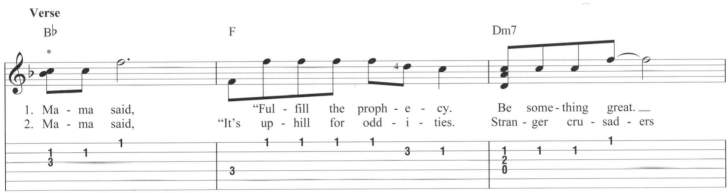

1. Ma - ma said, "Ful - fill the proph - e - cy. Be some - thing great. __
2. Ma - ma said, "It's up - hill for odd - i - ties. Stran - ger cru - sad - ers

Sung as written.

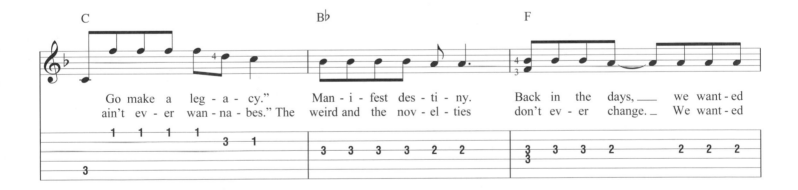

Go make a leg - a - cy." Man - i - fest des - ti - ny. Back in the days, __ we want - ed
ain't ev - er wan - na - bes." The weird and the nov - el - ties don't ev - er change. _ We want - ed

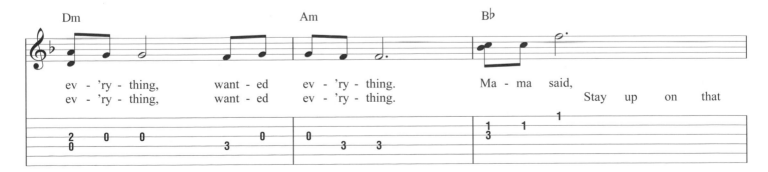

ev - 'ry - thing, want - ed ev - 'ry - thing. Ma - ma said,
ev - 'ry - thing, want - ed ev - 'ry - thing. Stay up on that

Burn your bi - o - graph - ies. Re - write your his - to - ry. Light up your wild - est dreams."
rise, stay up on that rise and nev - er come down, oh. _____

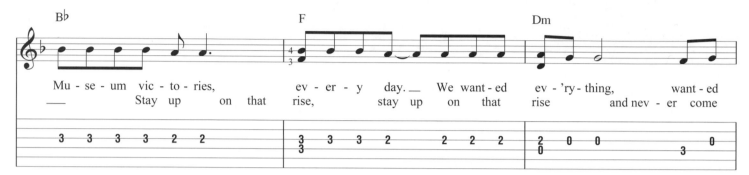

Mu - se - um vic - to - ries, ev - er - y day. ___ We want - ed ev - 'ry - thing, want - ed
___ Stay up on that rise, stay up on that rise and nev - er come

Pre-Chorus

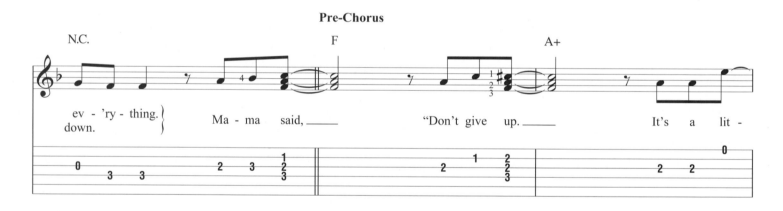

ev - 'ry - thing.⎫ Ma - ma said, _____ "Don't give up. _____ It's a lit -
down. ⎭

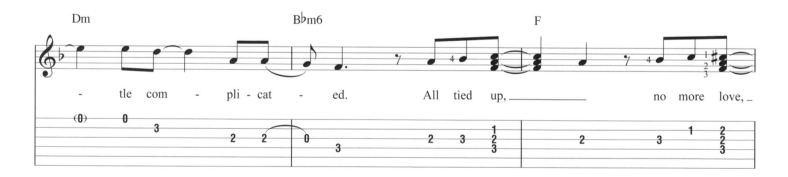

- tle com - pli - cat - ed. All tied up, _____ no more love, __

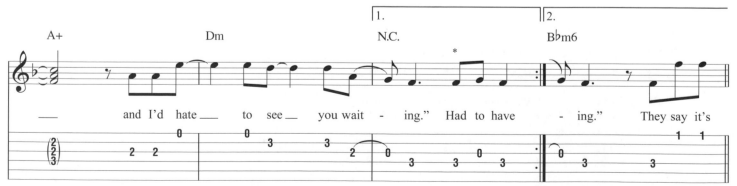

___ and I'd hate ___ to see ___ you wait - ing." Had to have - ing." They say it's

*Sung one octave higher.

Bridge

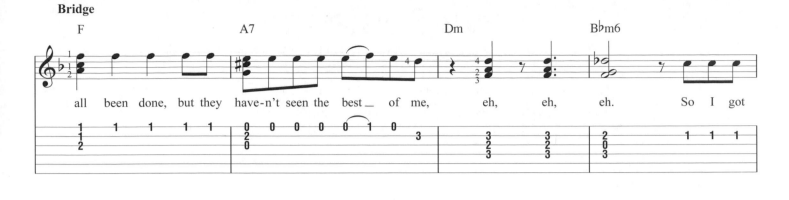

all been done, but they have-n't seen the best __ of me, eh, eh, eh. So I got

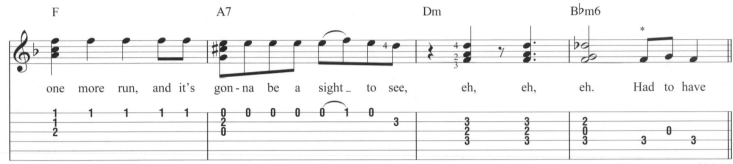

one more run, and it's gon-na be a sight __ to see, eh, eh, eh. Had to have

*Sung one octave higher.

Chorus

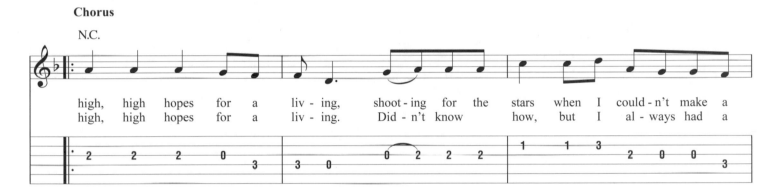

high, high hopes for a liv - ing, shoot - ing for the stars when I could-n't make a
high, high hopes for a liv - ing. Did - n't know how, but I al - ways had a

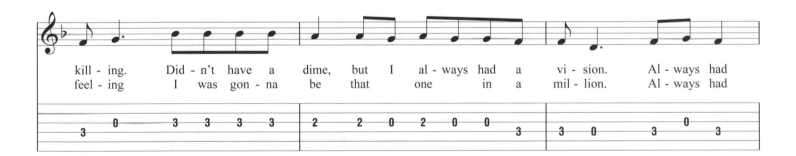

kill - ing. Did - n't have a dime, but I al - ways had a vi - sion. Al - ways had
feel - ing I was gon - na be that one in a mil - lion. Al - ways had

1.   2.   *D.S. al Fine*

high, high hopes. _____ Had to have _____ Had to have
high, high hopes. _____

17

Love Someone

Words and Music by Lukas Forchhammer, Morten Ristorp, Morten Pilegaard, Jaramye Daniels, Don Stefano, David LaBrel and James Ghaleb

smile. I'd stop the world if it gave us time.

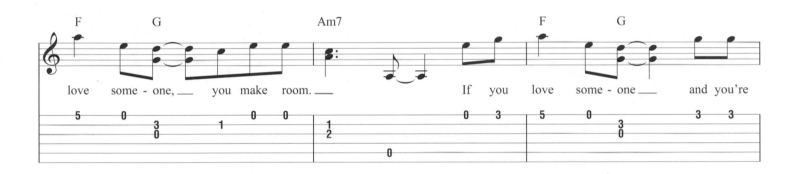

Chorus

'Cause when you love some - one, ___ you o - pen up ___ your heart. When you

love some - one, ___ you make room. ___ If you love some - one ___ and you're

not a - fraid ___ to lose 'em, you prob -'ly nev - er loved some - one ___ like I do. ___

3rd time, To Coda

___ You prob -'ly nev - er loved some - one ___ like I do. ___

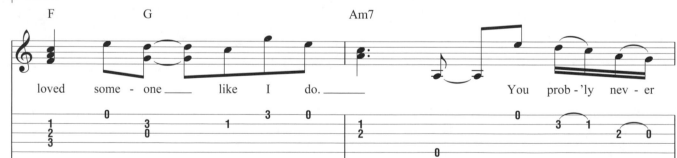

*Let chords ring, next 2 meas.

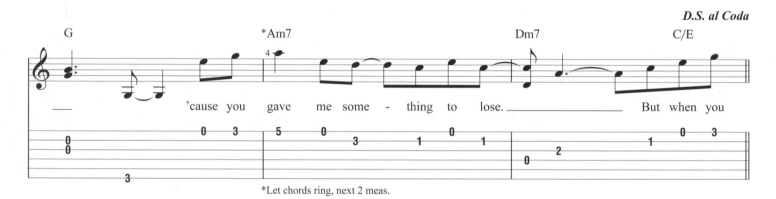

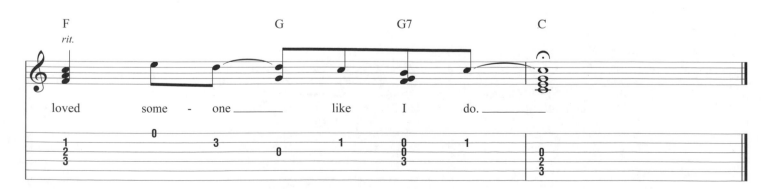

Millionaire

Words and Music by Kevin Welch

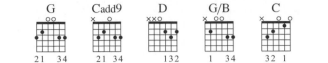

*Capo III

Strum Pattern: 1, 6
Pick Pattern: 4

Intro
Moderately slow, in

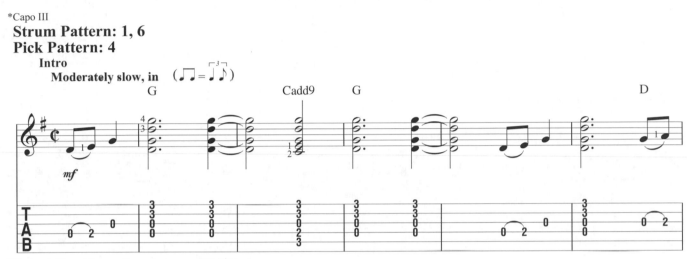

*Optional: To match recording, place capo at 3rd fret.

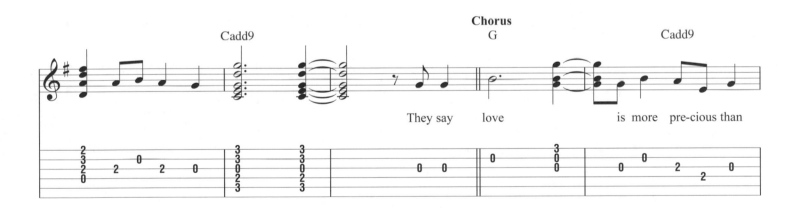

They say   love   is more pre-cious than

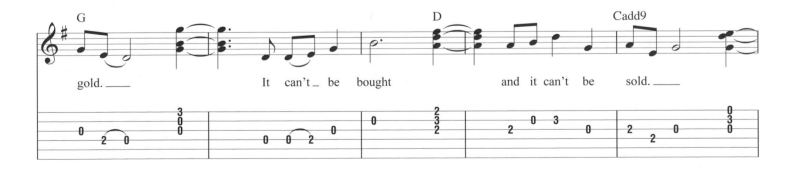

gold. ___   It   can't _ be   bought   and it can't be   sold. ___

I got love _____ e-nough to spare. _ That _ makes

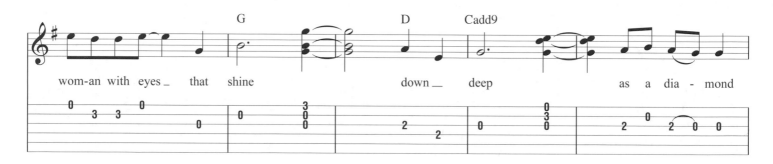

me a mil - lion - aire.

%Verse

1. I got a
2., 3. *See additional lyrics*

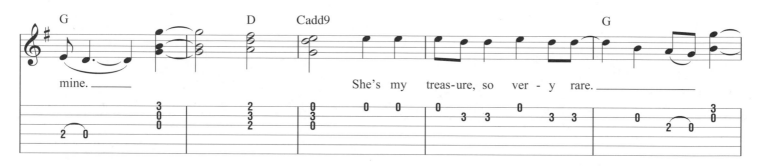

wom-an with eyes _ that shine down _ deep as a dia - mond mine. _____

She's my treas-ure, so ver - y rare. _____

She made me _____ a mil - lion - aire. _

1.

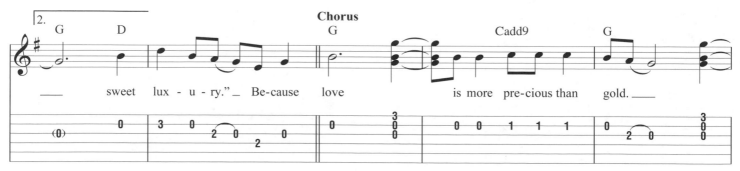

2.

_ sweet lux - u - ry." Be-cause love is more pre-cious than gold. _

Chorus

To Coda

D.S. al Coda
(take 2nd ending)

Coda

Additional Lyrics

2. When we ride around, ride around this old town
In my beat-up car with the windows down,
People look at her and they look at me
And say, "That boy is sure living in luxury, sweet luxury."

3. When her kisses fall from ev'rywhere,
Like riches on a millionaire,
When my pockets are empty and my cupboard is bare,
I still feel like a millionaire.

Natural

Words and Music by Dan Reynolds, Wayne Sermon, Ben McKee, Daniel Platzman, Justin Trantor, Mattias Larsson and Robin Fredricksson

Strum Pattern: 6
Pick Pattern: 1

Intro
Moderately, in 2

1. Well, you hold _ the line _____ when ev-'ry one of them is giv-ing
2. *See additional lyrics*

up and giv-ing in, tell me. In this house of mine, ___ noth-ing ev-er comes with-out a

con-se-quence or cost, tell me. Will the stars _ a-lign? _____ Will heav-en step in, will it

save us from our sin, will it? 'Cause this house __ of mine ____ stands strong. ___

Pre-Chorus

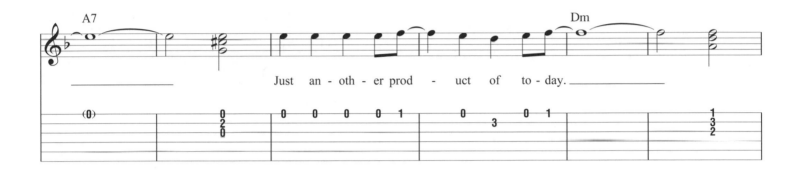

That's the price you pay. _____ Leave be-hind your heart - ache, cast a - way. __

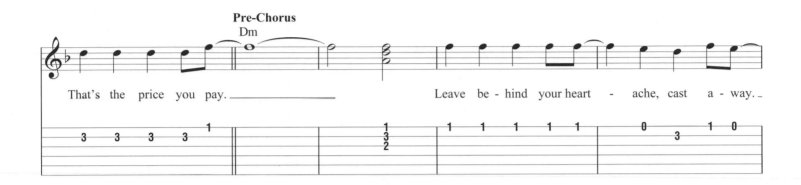

_____ Just an-oth-er prod - uct of to-day. _____

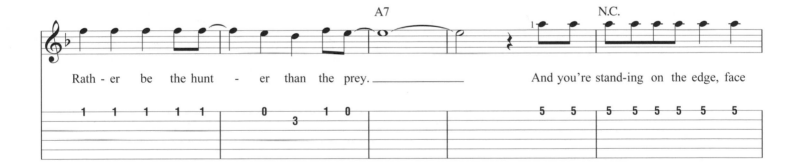

Rath - er be the hunt - er than the prey. _____ And you're stand-ing on the edge, face

Chorus

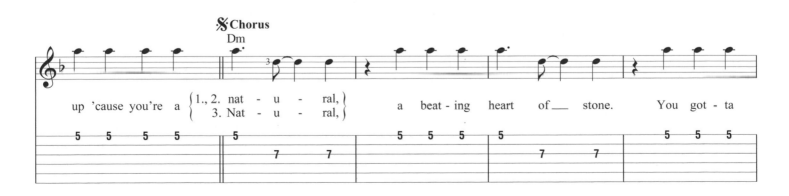

up 'cause you're a { 1., 2. nat - u - ral, / 3. Nat - u - ral, } a beat-ing heart of __ stone. You got - ta

3rd time, To Coda

26

Gon - na make it. I'm gon - na make it.

Coda

Outro

nat - u - ral.

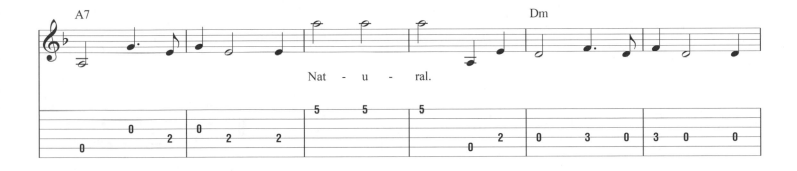

Nat - u - ral.

Yeah, you're a nat - u - ral.

Additional Lyrics

2. Will somebody let me see the light within the dark trees' shadows and
What's happening? Looking through the glass, find the wrong within the past knowing,
Oh, we are the youth. Call out to the beast, not a word without the peace, facing
A bit of truth, the truth. That's the price you pay.

Shallow

from A STAR IS BORN

Words and Music by Stefani Germanotta, Mark Ronson, Andrew Wyatt and Anthony Rossomando

where they can't hurt __ us. We're far from the shal - low now. _____ In the shal, -al

*Sung as written.

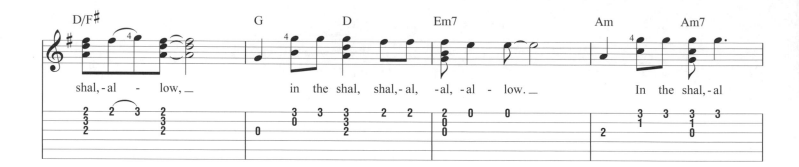

shal, -al - low, __ in the shal, shal, -al, -al, -al low. __ In the shal, -al

To Coda ⊕

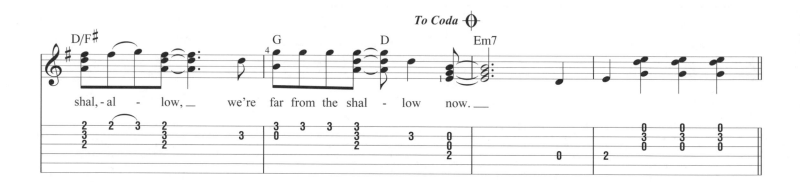

shal, -al - low, __ we're far from the shal - low now. __

Bridge

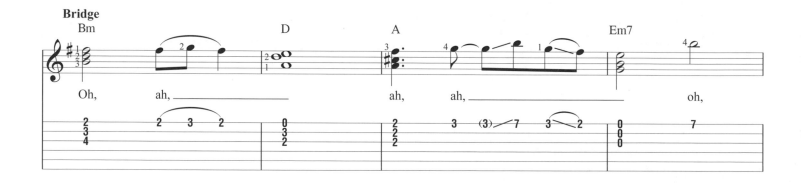

Oh, ah, _____ ah, ah, _____ oh,

D.S. al Coda ⊕ **Coda**

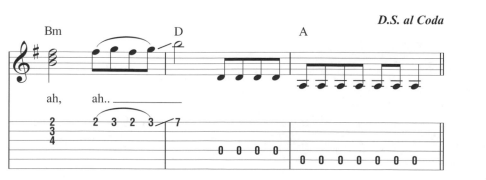

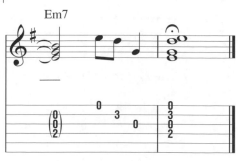

ah, ah.. _____

She Got the Best of Me

Words and Music by Robert Snyder, Luke Combs and Channing Wilson

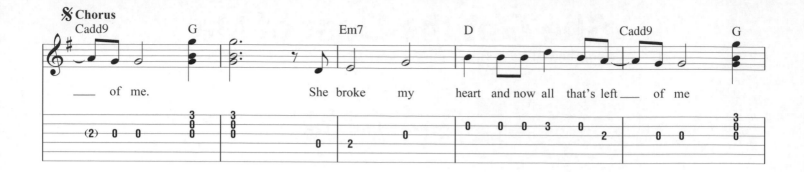

_ of me.   She broke my   heart and now all that's left __ of me

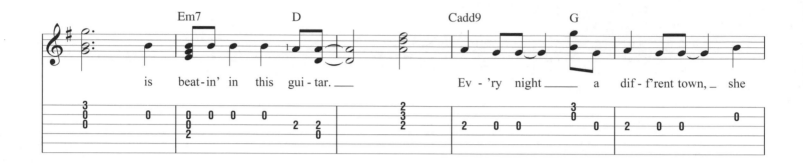

is beat-in' in this gui - tar. __   Ev - 'ry night ____ a dif - f'rent town, _ she

3rd time, To Coda ⊕

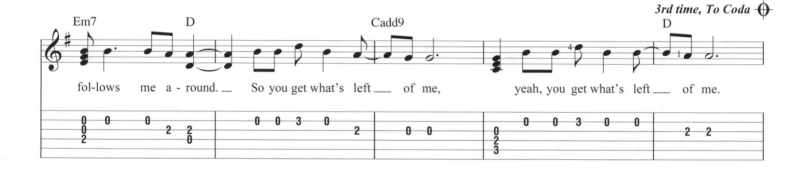

fol-lows me a - round. __ So you get what's left __ of me,   yeah, you get what's left __ of me.

1.
Interlude

'Cause she got the best __ of me.

2.
Bridge

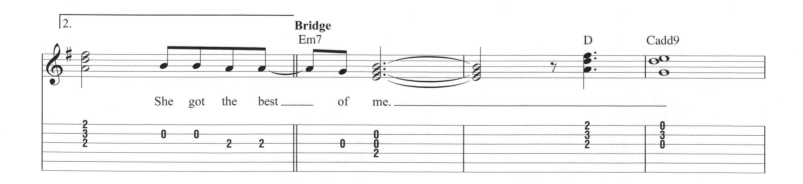

She got the best _____ of me. _____

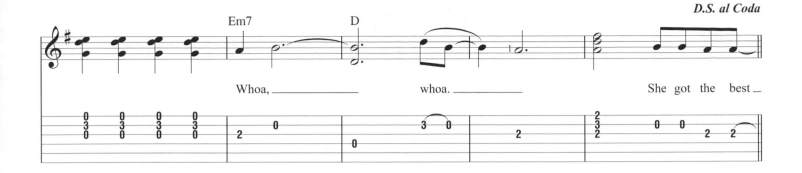

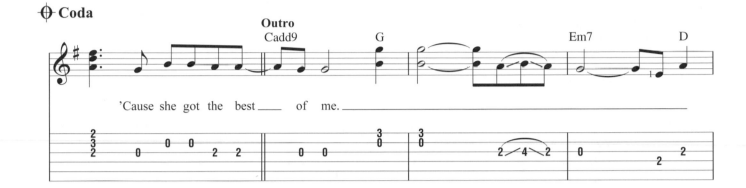

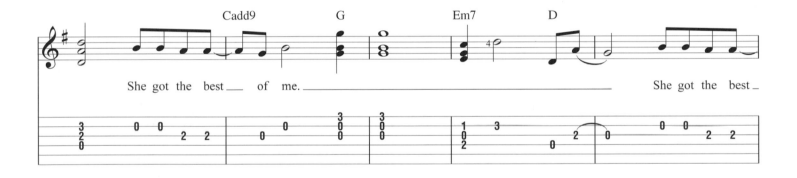

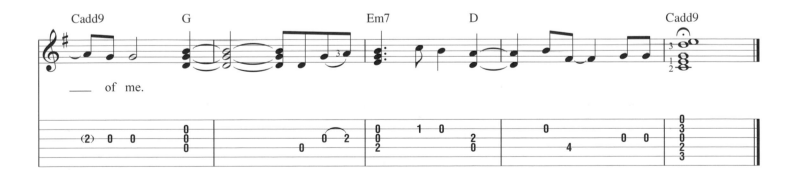

Additional Lyrics

2. I picked myself up off the floor and found something new worth living for
   In a old, dusty, hand-me-down six-string and a couple chords.
   I'm getting over her a little more with every song,
   So y'all sing along.

Shotgun

Words and Music by George Barnett, Joel Laslett Pott and Fred Gibson

*Tune down 1 step:
(low to high) D-G-C-F-A-D

Strum Pattern: 5
Pick Pattern: 1

Intro
Moderately

*Optional: To match recording, tune down 1 step.

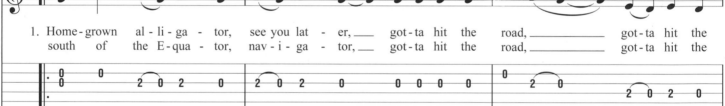

Verse

1. Home-grown al-i-ga-tor, see you lat-er, ___ got-ta hit the road, ___ got-ta hit the
south of the E-qua-tor, nav-i-ga-tor, ___ got-ta hit the road, ___ got-ta hit the

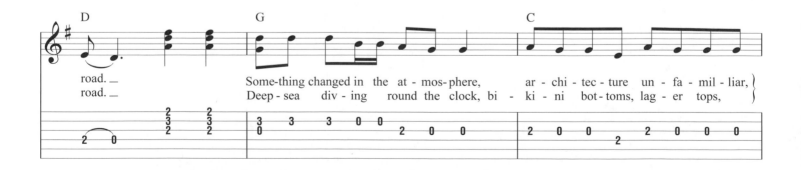

road. ___ Some-thing changed in the at-mos-phere, ar-chi-tec-ture un-fa-mil-liar,
road. ___ Deep-sea div-ing round the clock, bi-ki-ni bot-toms, lag-er tops,

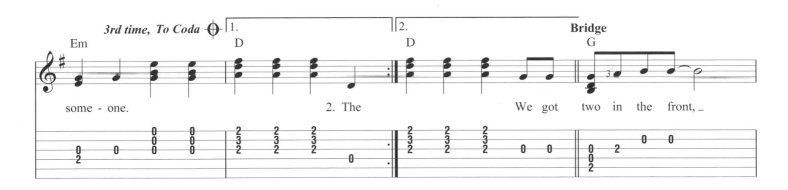

two in the back, __ sail - ing a - long __ and we don't look back. _____

Interlude

G   C   Em   *D.S. al Coda*   D

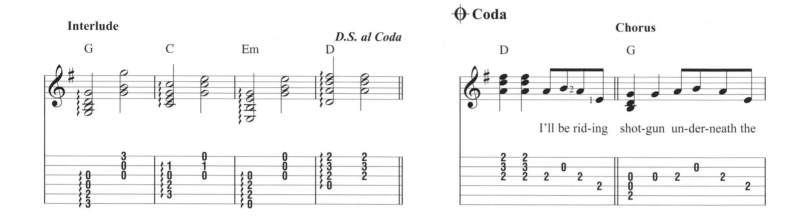

✠ **Coda**

Chorus

D   G

I'll be rid-ing shot-gun un-der-neath the

C   Em   D   G   C

hot sun, feel-ing like a some-one.   I'll be rid-ing shot-gun un-der-neath the hot sun, feel-ing like a

Outro

Em   D   G   C   Em   D   *Repeat and fade*

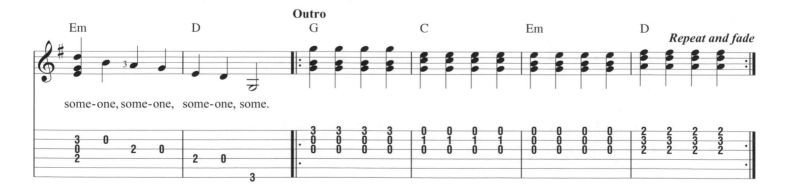

some-one, some-one, some-one, some.

Speechless

Words and Music by Dan Smyers, Shay Mooney, Jordan Reynolds and Laura Veltz

*Tune down 1/2 step:

(low to high) Eb-Ab-Db-Gb-Bb-Eb

Strum Pattern: 6

Pick Pattern: 4

*Optional: To match recording, tune down 1/2 step.

Pre-Chorus

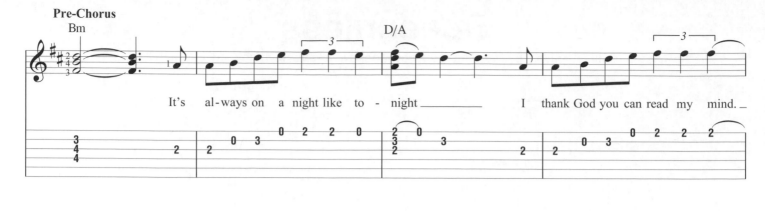

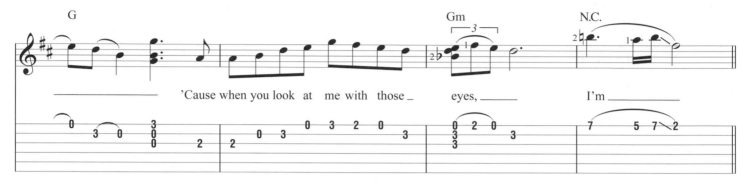

Chorus

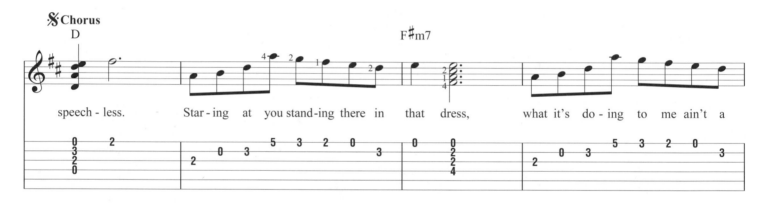

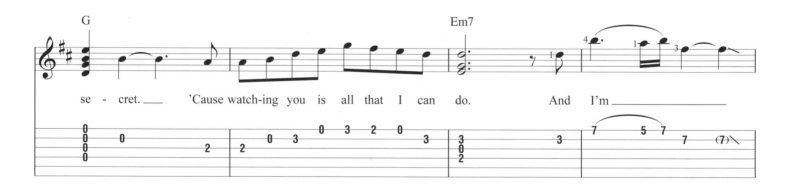

⊕ Coda
Guitar Solo

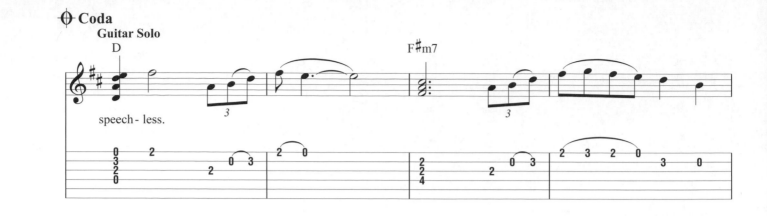

speech - less.

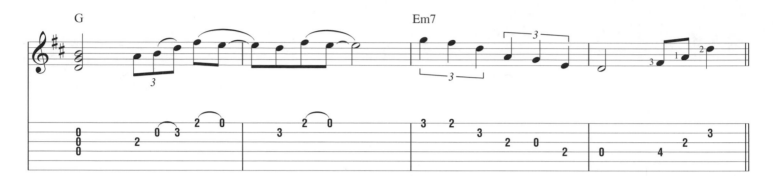

Pre-Chorus

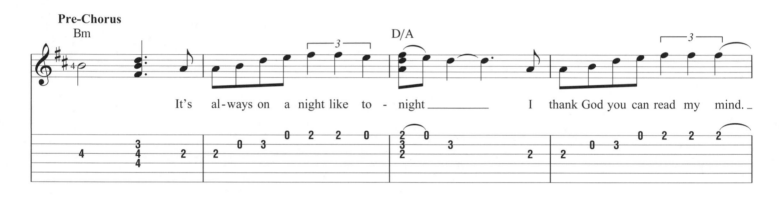

It's al-ways on a night like to - night_____ I thank God you can read my mind.

_____ 'Cause when you look at me with those _ eyes, _____ I'm

Chorus

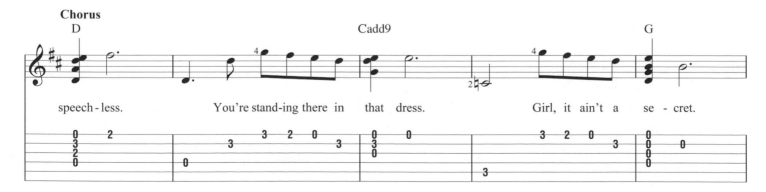

speech - less. You're stand-ing there in that dress. Girl, it ain't a se - cret.

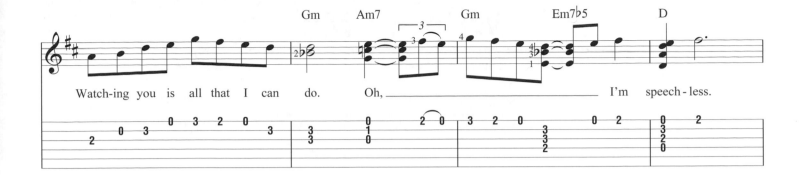

Watch-ing you is all that I can do. Oh, _____ I'm speech-less.

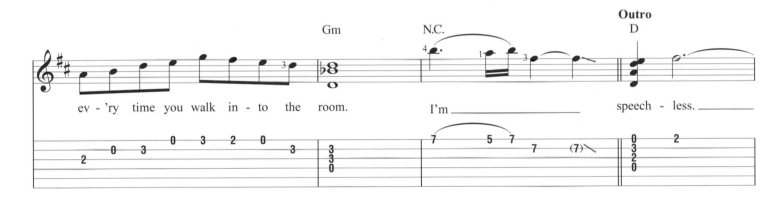

You al-read-y know that you're my weak-ness. Af-ter all this time, I'm just as nerv-ous _____

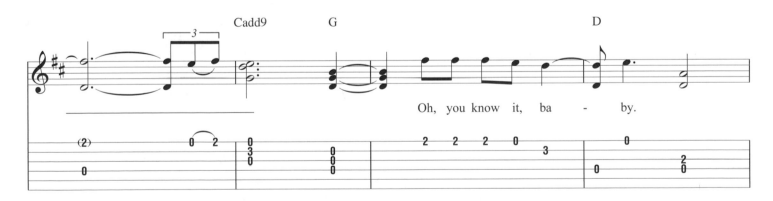

ev-'ry time you walk in-to the room. I'm _____ speech-less. _____

Outro

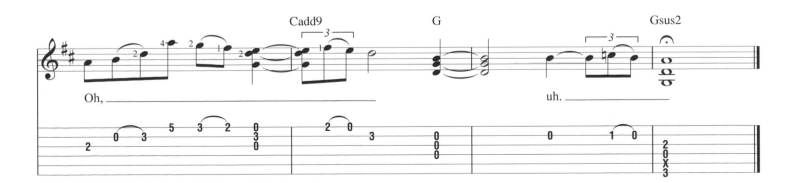

_____ Oh, you know it, ba - by.

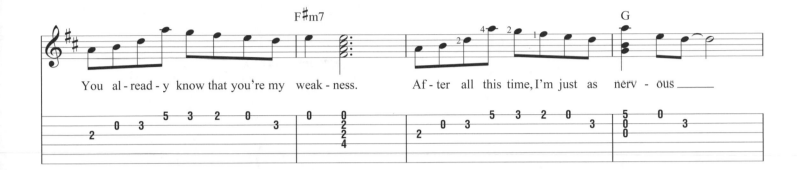

Oh, _____ uh. _____

Without Me

Words and Music by Ashley Frangipane, Brittany Amaradio, Carl Rosen,
Justin Timberlake, Scott Storch, Louis Bell, Amy Allen and Timothy Mosley

*Tune down 1/2 step:

(low to high) Eb-Ab-Db-Gb-Bb-Eb

Strum Pattern: 6
Pick Pattern: 5

*Optional: To match recording, tune down 1/2 step.

*Sung one octave higher.

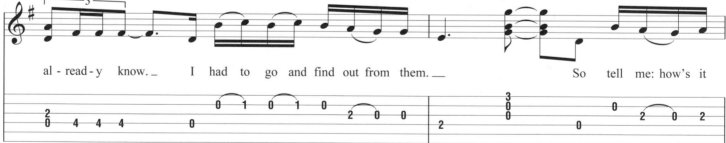

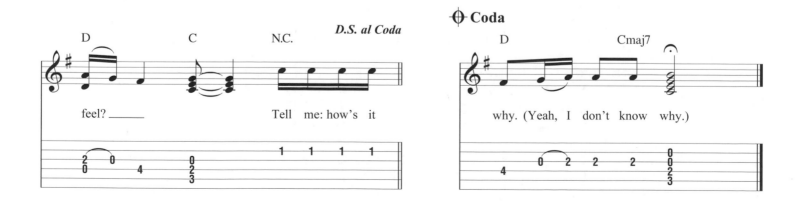

You Say

Words and Music by Lauren Daigle, Jason Ingram and Paul Mabury

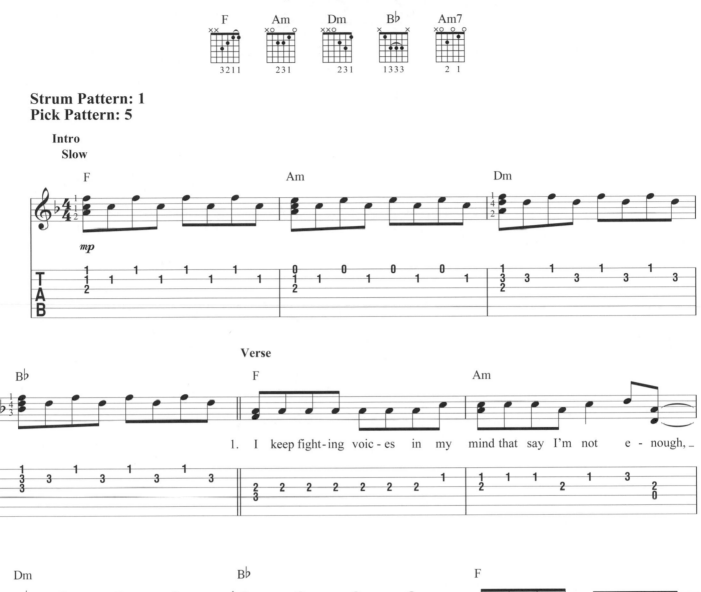

Strum Pattern: 1
Pick Pattern: 5

Intro
Slow

1. I keep fight-ing voic-es in my mind that say I'm not e - nough, _

ev - 'ry sin - gle lie that tells me

I will nev - er meas - ure up. _____

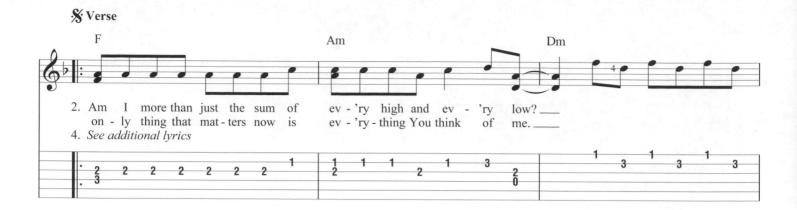

2. Am   I   more than   just   the   sum   of   ev - 'ry   high   and   ev - 'ry   low? ___
on - ly   thing   that   mat - ters   now   is   ev - 'ry - thing   You   think   of   me. ___
4. *See additional lyrics*

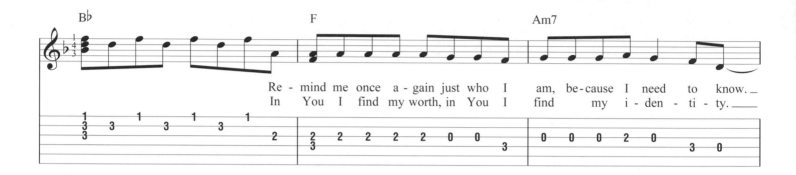

Re - mind   me   once   a - gain   just   who   I   am,   be-cause   I   need   to   know. __
In   You   I   find   my   worth,   in   You   I   find   my   i - den - ti - ty. ___

Chorus

Ooh,   oh. ___   You   say   I   am   loved   when   I   can't   feel   a

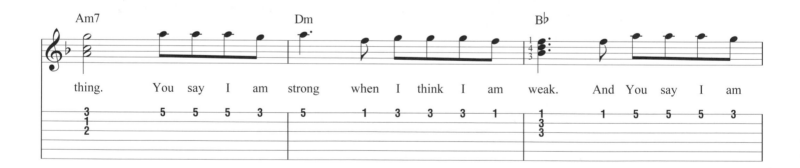

thing.   You   say   I   am   strong   when   I   think   I   am   weak.   And   You   say   I   am

held   when   I   am   fall - ing   short.   And   when   I   don't   be - long,   oh,   You   say   I   am

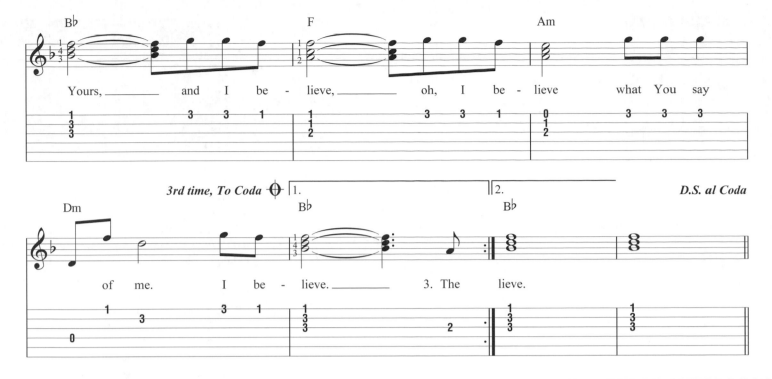

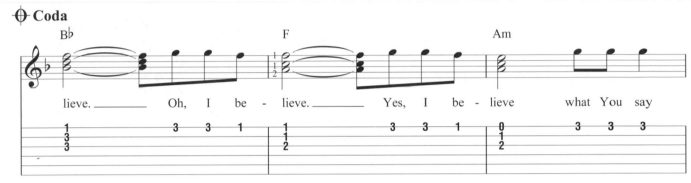

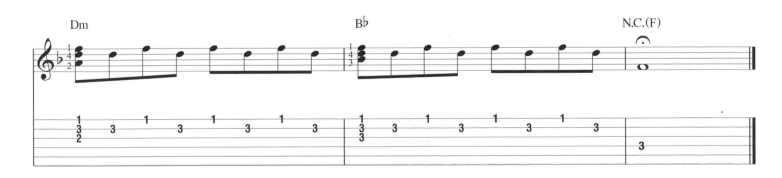

Additional Lyrics

4. Taking all I have, and now I'm laying it at Your feet.
You'll have ev'ry failure, God. You'll have ev'ry victory.

EASY GUITAR WITH NOTES & TAB

This series features simplified arrangements with notes, tab, chord charts, and strum and pick patterns.

MIXED FOLIOS

00702287	Acoustic	$16.99
00702002	Acoustic Rock Hits for Easy Guitar	$14.99
00702166	All-Time Best Guitar Collection	$19.99
00702232	Best Acoustic Songs for Easy Guitar	$14.99
00119835	Best Children's Songs	$16.99
00702233	Best Hard Rock Songs	$14.99
00703055	The Big Book of Nursery Rhymes & Children's Songs	$16.99
00322179	The Big Easy Book of Classic Rock Guitar	$24.95
00698978	Big Christmas Collection	$17.99
00702394	Bluegrass Songs for Easy Guitar	$12.99
00703387	Celtic Classics	$14.99
00224808	Chart Hits of 2016-2017	$14.99
00702149	Children's Christian Songbook	$9.99
00702237	Christian Acoustic Favorites	$12.95
00702028	Christmas Classics	$8.99
00101779	Christmas Guitar	$14.99
00702185	Christmas Hits	$10.99
00702141	Classic Rock	$8.95
00702203	CMT's 100 Greatest Country Songs	$27.95
00702283	The Contemporary Christian Collection	$16.99

00702239	Country Classics for Easy Guitar	$19.99
00702282	Country Hits of 2009–2010	$14.99
00702257	Easy Acoustic Guitar Songs	$14.99
00702280	Easy Guitar Tab White Pages	$29.99
00702041	Favorite Hymns for Easy Guitar	$10.99
00140841	4-Chord Hymns for Guitar	$9.99
00702281	4 Chord Rock	$10.99
00126894	Frozen	$14.99
00702286	Glee	$16.99
00699374	Gospel Favorites	$16.99
00122138	The Grammy Awards® Record of the Year 1958-2011	$19.99
00702160	The Great American Country Songbook	$16.99
00702050	Great Classical Themes for Easy Guitar	$8.99
00702116	Greatest Hymns for Guitar	$10.99
00702184	Guitar Instrumentals	$9.95
00148030	Halloween Guitar Songs	$14.99
00702273	Irish Songs	$12.99
00702275	Jazz Favorites for Easy Guitar	$15.99
00702274	Jazz Standards for Easy Guitar	$15.99
00702162	Jumbo Easy Guitar Songbook	$19.99
00702258	Legends of Rock	$14.99

00702189	MTV's 100 Greatest Pop Songs	$24.95
00702272	1950s Rock	$15.99
00702271	1960s Rock	$15.99
00702270	1970s Rock	$15.99
00702269	1980s Rock	$15.99
00702268	1990s Rock	$15.99
00109725	Once	$14.99
00702187	Selections from O Brother Where Art Thou?	$15.99
00702178	100 Songs for Kids	$14.99
00702515	Pirates of the Caribbean	$14.99
00702125	Praise and Worship for Guitar	$10.99
00702285	Southern Rock Hits	$12.99
00121535	30 Easy Celtic Guitar Solos	$14.99
00702220	Today's Country Hits	$9.95
00121900	Today's Women of Pop & Rock	$14.99
00283786	Top Hits of 2018	$14.99
00702294	Top Worship Hits	$15.99
00702255	VH1's 100 Greatest Hard Rock Songs	$27.99
00702175	VH1's 100 Greatest Songs of Rock and Roll	$24.95
00702253	Wicked	$12.99

ARTIST COLLECTIONS

00702267	AC/DC for Easy Guitar	$15.99
00702598	Adele for Easy Guitar	$15.99
00702040	Best of the Allman Brothers	$15.99
00702865	J.S. Bach for Easy Guitar	$14.99
00702169	Best of The Beach Boys	$12.99
00702292	The Beatles — 1	$19.99
00125796	Best of Chuck Berry	$14.99
00702201	The Essential Black Sabbath	$12.95
02501615	Zac Brown Band — The Foundation	$16.99
02501621	Zac Brown Band — You Get What You Give	$16.99
00702043	Best of Johnny Cash	$16.99
00702090	Eric Clapton's Best	$12.99
00702086	Eric Clapton — from the Album Unplugged	$10.95
00702202	The Essential Eric Clapton	$14.99
00702250	blink-182 — Greatest Hits	$15.99
00702053	Best of Patsy Cline	$14.99
00702229	The Very Best of Creedence Clearwater Revival	$15.99
00702145	Best of Jim Croce	$15.99
00702278	Crosby, Stills & Nash	$12.99
00702219	David Crowder*Band Collection	$12.95
14042809	Bob Dylan	$14.99
00702276	Fleetwood Mac — Easy Guitar Collection	$14.99
00139462	The Very Best of Grateful Dead	$15.99
00702136	Best of Merle Haggard	$12.99
00702227	Jimi Hendrix — Smash Hits	$14.99
00702288	Best of Hillsong United	$12.99
00702236	Best of Antonio Carlos Jobim	$14.99
00702245	Elton John — Greatest Hits 1970–2002	$14.99

00129855	Jack Johnson	$15.99
00702204	Robert Johnson	$10.99
00702234	Selections from Toby Keith — 35 Biggest Hits	$12.95
00702003	Kiss	$10.99
00110578	Best of Kutless	$12.99
00702216	Lynyrd Skynyrd	$15.99
00702182	The Essential Bob Marley	$14.94
00146081	Maroon 5	$14.99
00121925	Bruno Mars – Unorthodox Jukebox	$12.99
00702248	Paul McCartney — All the Best	$14.99
00702129	Songs of Sarah McLachlan	$12.95
00125484	The Best of MercyMe	$12.99
02501316	Metallica — Death Magnetic	$19.99
00702209	Steve Miller Band — Young Hearts (Greatest Hits)	$12.95
00124167	Jason Mraz	$15.99
00702096	Best of Nirvana	$15.99
00702211	The Offspring — Greatest Hits	$12.95
00138026	One Direction	$14.99
00702030	Best of Roy Orbison	$14.99
00702144	Best of Ozzy Osbourne	$14.99
00702279	Tom Petty	$12.99
00102911	Pink Floyd	$16.99
00702139	Elvis Country Favorites	$14.99
00702293	The Very Best of Prince	$15.99
00699415	Best of Queen for Guitar	$14.99
00109279	Best of R.E.M.	$14.99
00702208	Red Hot Chili Peppers — Greatest Hits	$14.99

00198960	The Rolling Stones	$16.99
00174793	The Very Best of Santana	$14.99
00702196	Best of Bob Seger	$12.95
00146046	Ed Sheeran	$14.99
00702252	Frank Sinatra — Nothing But the Best	$12.99
00702010	Best of Rod Stewart	$16.99
00702049	Best of George Strait	$14.99
00702259	Taylor Swift for Easy Guitar	$15.99
00702260	Taylor Swift — Fearless	$14.99
00139727	Taylor Swift — 1989	$17.99
00115960	Taylor Swift — Red	$16.99
00253667	Taylor Swift — Reputation	$17.99
00702290	Taylor Swift — Speak Now	$15.99
00702226	Chris Tomlin — See the Morning	$12.95
00148643	Train	$14.99
00702427	U2 — 18 Singles	$16.99
00702108	Best of Stevie Ray Vaughan	$16.99
00702123	Best of Hank Williams	$14.99
00702111	Stevie Wonder — Guitar Collection	$9.95
00702228	Neil Young — Greatest Hits	$15.99
00119133	Neil Young — Harvest	$14.99
00702188	Essential ZZ Top	$14.99

Prices, contents and availability subject to change without notice.

Visit Hal Leonard online at
www.halleonard.com

1118
306